THROUGH THE FIRE

THROUGH THE FIRE 🔥:

DELIVERANCE FROM WITCHCRAFT, CURSES, NARCISSISM, AND THE JEZEBEL SPIRIT

By Antoinette Lewis

COPYRIGHT

Copyright © 2022 Antoinette Lewis. All rights reserved. Published by PurposeHouse Publishing, Columbia, Maryland. Cover Design by PurposeHouse Publishing. Printed in the USA.

No part of this publication may be reproduced or distributed in any form or by any means or stored in a database or retrieval system without the prior written permission of the author.

ISBN: 978-1-957190-05-1
Scripture taken from The Holy Bible: Easy-to-Read Version (ERV), International Edition
© 2013, 2016 by Bible League International and used by permission.

Scripture quotations marked "KJV" are taken from the Holy Bible, King James Version (Public Domain).

Scripture quotations taken from The Holy Bible, New International Version® NIV ® Copyright © 2011 by Biblica, Inc. TM. Used by permission. All rights reserved worldwide.

Scripture taken from the New King James Version®. Copyright © 1982 by Thomas Nelson. Used by permission. All rights reserved.

Scripture quotations marked (NLT) are taken from the Holy Bible, New Living Translation, copyright ©1996, 2004, 2015 by Tyndale House Foundation. Used by permission of Tyndale House Publishers, Carol Stream, Illinois 60188. All rights reserved.

CONTENTS

Introduction 1

Chapter 1: Ignorance 7

Chapter 2: Generational Curses 33

Chapter 3: Narcissism 55

Chapter 4: Jezebel 69

INTRODUCTION

You are reading something precious, the manifestation of a word spoken to me, a woman who never thought she was a writer and, for a season, never thought God would use her again. But somehow, God spoke to me. He told me to write when I was in transition, my marriage was in separation, and guilt spoke louder than his love. I didn't know my marriage would be restored, and I certainly did not expect such valuable lessons on deliverance to emerge from my sin and shame. Yet, God proved himself to be sovereign.

The Lord told me to write in 2019. I had my doubts, yet, in response, I bought ten ISBNs, the international registration number required to publish a book. That may not seem significant, but at the time, I was separated from my husband and in an adulterous relationship. My husband and I never officially divorced and had been married for eighteen years. We separated for seven years before getting back together officially in 2021. So, my husband and I separated in 2014, I started seeing someone from my job in 2018, and God spoke to me to write in 2019. The year 2020 was the year God opened my eyes and brought me back into a relationship with him, and my husband and I reunited in 2021. Yes, I have come to realize God's sovereign, awesome delivering power, and that's the reason I wrote this book.

While I was with the guy from my job, I was sure I was on my way to hell. I felt trapped—in chains and bondage—but didn't fully understand why. I was convinced God could never use me again. You see, when I was a teenager, I would receive dreams from God and see things others could not see. But the dreams stopped: they ceased, and I felt so far away from God.

But then something happened. God started speaking to me about the guy I was in adultery with through dreams. Around this time, my husband started coming back around. Subsequently, I had another dream that my husband and I were at a wedding getting married. It was 2020, and my spiritual eyes were open again. Praise Jesus! God was restoring me. I was like a parched, thirsty woman at a well. I began to read the Word; I read books and gained information on the things that had happened to me in that adulterous relationship, and again, God said, "Write."

The adulterous relationship had become an idol, so I searched Google for things like "worshipping other gods." I knew what I had been doing was absolutely wrong. When I was around this person, I saw something evil, so I ran, and I was like, "Okay, God. What are you saying?" The dreams about me and this person intensified. At the time, I was not familiar with Matthew 17:21, but the Holy Spirit led me to fast for ten days without food or water.

> HOWBEIT THIS KIND GOETH NOT OUT BUT BY PRAYER AND FASTING. (MATTHEW 17:21 KJV)

> BUT THAT KIND OF SPIRIT COMES OUT ONLY WITH PRAYER AND FASTING. (MATTHEW 17:21 ERV)

I had no idea what the man I had entangled myself with was carrying. Through him and my deliverance from him, I learned about the spirits of narcissism and Jezebel. I learned about hexes, curses, and spells. Through adultery, I had allowed myself to be entrapped and entangled by a worker of evil. His craftiness, coupled with my bloodline issues, were a destructive combination. But I was also learning about God's power to deliver. I know without a doubt, that if he can do it for me, he can do it for someone else.

I even had to ask the Lord to show me how to fast. Whenever I was fasting, and God would say, "Come off the fast," I would not know if it was me, God, or the devil speaking. By the mercy of God, I got through it. I started seeking God heavily, and he led me to a church home. And I had actually met the First Lady in 2017 in training together on our job. God is sovereign and orders our steps.

The Lord has brought me through the fire, and I want people to know how he did it and that he can do it for them too. Although there are many Christian books, I wrote this book to help readers identify the spiritual forces behind the issues plaguing them and target the root of the problems that want to keep them bound. This book is written to be a road to deliverance and staying delivered. Once we recognize and identify our "bad" habits, we can turn them around. You see, I had labeled my adultery as a "bad habit," not knowing it was leading me down a slippery slope. Thank God for deliverance, and our Lord and Savior, Jesus, gets the glory. Through this book, may the Holy Spirit lead you and help you make connections to the spiritual implications behind what's taken place in your life, bloodline, and relationships.

CHAPTER 1: IGNORANCE

> MY PEOPLE ARE DESTROYED FOR LACK OF KNOWLEDGE... (HOSEA 4:6A KJV)

> ...BUT THROUGH KNOWLEDGE SH ALL THE JUST BE DELIVERED. (PROVERBS 11:9B KJV)

When people hear the words witch or witchcraft, they picture an old woman with a boil on her nose standing over a black cauldron or chanting something silly like "hocus pocus." We participate in Halloween, we laugh and joke at scary movies, and we watch so-called children's movies full of witchcraft and divination. The media has desensitized us to the realities of witchcraft and the potency of the powers that back its activities. The Wiccans and satanists are organized, recognized religions that are growing in number every day in the United States (US). According to a 2018 article by Pew Research, there were an estimated 1.5 million Wicca or Pagans in the US, which means that witches outnumber Presbyterians in America.[1] And many young people are being converted, choosing to identify with witchcraft rather than traditional, mainline religion. The melting pot of nationalities in the US has brought with it a melting pot of religions, rituals, and witchcraft practices veiled as culture. And we go to work daily with witches and warlocks and don't even know it. We are completely unsuspecting and unaware of their

---

[1] Pew Research Center. "Religious Landscape Study." Pewresearch.org. Accessed July 6, 2022. https://www.pewresearch.org/religion/religious-landscape-study/religious-denomination/pagan-or-wiccan/.

growth and prevalence in our society. Or at least, I was.

However, I now know that the Scriptures are loaded with instances and examples of witchcraft and God's power to deal with it. Here are some Scripture references from both the Old and New Testaments concerning witchcraft:

- For rebellion is as the sin of witchcraft, and stubbornness is as iniquity and idolatry. Because thou hast rejected the word of the Lord, he hath also rejected thee from being king. (1 Samuel 15:23 KJV)
- Manasseh also sacrificed his own sons in the fire in the valley of Ben-Hinnom. He practiced sorcery, divination, and witchcraft, and he consulted with mediums and psychics. He did much that was evil in the Lord's sight, arousing his anger. (2 Chronicles 33:6 NLT)
- Now the works of the flesh are manifest, which are these; Adultery, fornication,

uncleanness, lasciviousness, 20 Idolatry, *witchcraft*, hatred, variance, emulations, wrath, strife, seditions, heresies (Galatians 5:19-21 KJV, italics added)

- But there was a certain man, called Simon, which beforetime in the same city *used sorcery, and bewitched the people* of Samaria, giving out that himself was some great one: (Acts 8:9 KJV, italics added)

Though these examples exist and clearly indicate the presence of witchcraft in our world today, they are hardly ever the focus of a Sunday sermon. Sadly, most churches don't teach their members how to confront these forces of the enemy because the leaders themselves lack understanding or don't want to risk reduced offerings or offended membership. So, the average Christian is crippled—ignorant—when it comes to the dealings and operations of witchcraft and how to win the battle against them. Most believe that if I don't bother them, they won't bother me. But that couldn't be more wrong.

> Stay alert! Watch out for your great enemy, the devil. He prowls around like a roaring lion, looking for someone to devour. ⁹ Stand firm against him, and be strong in your faith. Remember that your family of believers all over the world is going through the same kind of suffering you are. (1 Peter 5:8-9 NLT)

The devil doesn't need an excuse to try to devour you. Unfortunately, I didn't realize that I was actually helping him to devour me. I was doing his work for him. We are instructed to stand against him and be strong in the faith. But who is teaching the body of believers to stand against witchcraft?

I wasn't a person who "actively" practiced witchcraft, so why then did it follow me? Questions like this began to flood my mind in 2020. This type of ignorance is what led me into a state of perishing, entangled in a relationship with a man who wielded witchcraft powers. In 2018, I met this guy at my job. Even though I was still married, my husband and I were separated, and I decided to pursue a "relationship" with this person. And just like I did with previous guys, I told him I was still married as if that was going to change the fact that I was an adulterous woman. I was already operating in sin and breaking many biblical laws, commands, and principles, such as the following:

- Thou shalt not commit adultery. (Exodus 20:14 KJV)
- Now concerning the things whereof ye wrote unto me: It is good for a man not to touch a woman. 2. Nevertheless, to avoid fornication, let every man have his own wife, and let every woman have her own husband. (1 Corinthians 7:1-2 KJV)

Of course, I ignored the conviction because, at the time, I allowed my fleshly desires to overtake me. And besides, I told myself I was living my "best life." I was walking in rebellion, which opened the door for witchcraft to oppress my life.

> Surely you know that your bodies are parts of Christ himself. So, I must never take

> what is part of Christ and join it to a prostitute! **16** The Scriptures say, "The two people will become one." So you should know that anyone who is joined with a prostitute becomes one with her in body. **17** But anyone who is joined with the Lord is one with him in spirit. **18** So run away from sexual sin. It involves the body in a way that no other sin does. So, if you commit sexual sin, you are sinning against your own body. **19** You should know that your body is a temple for the Holy Spirit that you received from God and that lives in you. You don't own yourselves. **20** God paid a very high price to make you his. So, honor God with your body. (1 Corinthians 6:15-20 ERV)

So, meeting this person was no accident: It was a setup. I had no idea I was assisting the enemy in orchestrating my own demise. By giving my adulterous partner access to my soul through sex, I was giving the enemy access to my soul. I now know and understand that the word of God will affect a person's life, whether aware, unaware, knowingly, or unknowingly. It will accomplish what it's set out to accomplish. Breaking any law or commandment of God has consequences, especially when we are walking in ignorance of the enemy's devices.

- Lest Satan should get an advantage of us: for we are not ignorant of his devices. (2 Corinthians 2:11 KJV)

The enemy knows the Word and will use it against the believer who lacks knowledge. So, everything that was happening was operating on legal grounds. This is one of the dangers of ignorance. The advantage the enemy was gaining was because of disobedience and ignorance.

The definition of ignorant *(adjective)* is:

1. lacking in knowledge or training; unlearned
2. lacking knowledge or information as to a particular subject or fact
3. uninformed; unaware.

4. due to or showing lack of knowledge or training[2]

And the definition of ignorance (*noun*) is:

1. the state or fact of being **ignorant**; lack of knowledge, learning, information, etc.[3]

As I said, I met this person in 2018, not knowing what he practiced or any of his religious beliefs. Unfortunately, so many Christians rush into relationships without taking the time to study and investigate the person. It is so dangerous, yet we often don't take the necessary time to know a person before opening up our emotions and giving our bodies to someone. The enemy uses loneliness, societal pressures, and sexual desires as tools to entrap us in dangerous, destructive relationships. God's mercy rescued me, but I don't want anyone

---

[2] Dictionary.com, s.v. "Definition of ignorant (adjective)," accessed July 6, 2022,
https://www.dictionary.com/browse/ignorant
[3] Dictionary.com, s.v. "Definition of ignorance (noun)," accessed July 6, 2022,
https://www.dictionary.com/browse/ignorance

to go through what I did before I experienced the Lord's restoration.

When the Lord began calling me back home, I would have many dreams and see things in the spiritual realm. Of course, I didn't tell anyone because I would have immediately been labeled as crazy or fanatic. So, I kept that part to myself until later. I realized the guy wasn't who he claimed he was, and neither was I. I left the relationship.

However, when I finally left, I had to fight not to return because, all of a sudden, I had uncontrollable urges to be with this person — emotionally, sexually, physically, and spiritually. At some point, I could hear this person call me. And I don't mean I could hear him calling me on the phone. I could hear him calling for me in my soul without him calling me on the phone. It was a serious tie and entanglement. I was being attacked from every corner and didn't see or understand why. This had never happened to me before. Or, if it did, I never paid full attention to it. In fact, I would just run to another person. But with this person, it was like a grip, hold, and bondage that did not want to let me go.

This time was different. After I was attacked from every angle and in every area of my life, I said to the Lord, "Something has to happen." It felt like I was dying. I heard these words, "These kinds come out but by prayer and fasting." So, I **Googled** these words and began reading the story in Matthew 17:21.

I then tried to fast. I fasted for ten days with no food or water and was still doing my daily duties. I heard the Lord say, "Come off," on the fourth day. Now, I know it was the Lord. It is not advisable to go without water for more than three days. But then, I didn't trust myself. I couldn't tell if it was my voice, the devil's voice, or if it was God's. So, I stayed on for ten days. On the eleventh day, I had to nurse myself like a baby. You definitely want to drink lots of water when fasting (no food).

As my walk with the Lord grew, I also grew in knowledge about the correct ways of fasting. Not only should you drink lots of water, but also replace the time you would have spent eating in prayer and the Word. Fasting is not about starving yourself but denying your flesh and filling yourself with more of God.

I had a strong urge to seek the Lord because of the things I saw and because I heard him (the Lord) call me. And thank God, there was so much relief after I fasted correctly. Something fell off my life; chains were falling and breaking. He promises results when we fast the right way. God himself lists some of the many benefits of fasting and the results we will get if we do it his way in Isaiah 58:

> 'We have fasted before you!' they say. 'Why aren't you impressed? We have been very hard on ourselves, and you don't even notice it!' "I will tell you why!" I respond. "It's because you are fasting to please yourselves. Even while you fast, you keep oppressing your workers. [4] What good is fasting when you keep on fighting and

quarreling? This kind of fasting will never get you anywhere with me. [5] You humble yourselves by going through the motions of penance, bowing your heads like reeds bending in the wind. You dress in burlap and cover yourselves with ashes. Is this what you call fasting? Do you really think this will please the LORD? [6] "No, this is the kind of fasting I want: Free those who are wrongly imprisoned; lighten the burden of those who work for you. Let the oppressed go free, and remove the chains that bind people. [7] Share your food with the hungry, and give shelter to the homeless. Give clothes to those who need them, and do not hide from relatives who need your help. [8] "Then your salvation will come like the dawn, and your wounds will quickly heal. Your godliness will lead you forward, and the glory of the LORD will protect you from behind. [9] Then when you call, the LORD will answer. 'Yes, I am here,' he will quickly reply. "Remove the heavy yoke of oppression. Stop pointing your finger and spreading vicious rumors! [10] Feed the hungry, and help those in trouble. Then your light will shine out from the darkness, and the darkness around you will be as bright as noon. [11] The LORD will guide you continually, giving you water when you are dry and restoring your strength. You will be like a well-watered garden, like an ever-flowing spring. ¹²Some of you will rebuild the deserted ruins of your cities. Then you will be known as a rebuilder of walls and a restorer of homes. (Isaiah 58:3-12 NLT)

Hallelujah! Through knowledge the just are delivered (Proverbs 11:9b KJV). As I continued seeking the Lord, fasting, and praying, I was going through a transformation and metamorphosis. I was being delivered. I'm certain my mom and sister thought I was losing my mind. Certainly, they thought, "Here's a woman who was clearly and openly sinning, and now she's talking about how she's hearing from the Lord." For better or worse, they heard all the dreams and messages the Lord gave me. In hindsight, I know they couldn't have fully understood me. But I was so excited, all the while in fight mode spiritually. I was coming out. I was being delivered.

Still, I was not fully equipped. At the time, I didn't know or understand the many ways of witchcraft.

I ignorantly thought it was a person simply mixing potions and casting spells. That happens too, but as it turns out, witchcraft also comes in the form of rebellion, manipulation, domination, and control. Anytime you alter or try to alter someone's destiny, try to control someone—any time you turn someone's "no" into your "yes," that is witchcraft. That is partly why Galatians 5:20 lists witchcraft as a work of the flesh. Many times, a person's unredeemed, fleshly, carnal desires are the root of manipulation and a desire to control the outcome of a situation. They don't want you to succeed, so they manipulate the situation. They don't want you to leave the relationship, so they manipulate your soul to try to maintain control. Their flesh wants power; they are greedy and will resort to any means necessary to satisfy that greed.

Remember when the Lord told Saul to go and kill everyone and everything from the Amalekite camp, but Saul didn't? He decided for his own selfish gain to keep the best sheep and cattle. The underlying issues were disobedience, manipulation, rebellion, selfishness, and greed. And all these things oppose God's word and will.

> And the LORD sent thee on a journey, and said, Go and utterly destroy the sinners the Amalekites, and fight against them until they be consumed. [19] Wherefore then didst thou not obey the voice of the LORD, but didst fly upon the spoil, and didst evil in the sight of the LORD? [20] And Saul said unto Samuel, Yea, I have obeyed the voice of the LORD, and have gone the way which the LORD sent me, and have brought Agag the king of Amalek, and have utterly destroyed the Amalekites. [21] But the people took of the spoil, sheep and oxen, the chief of the things which should have been utterly destroyed, to sacrifice unto the LORD thy God in Gilgal. [22] And Samuel said, Hath the LORD as great delight in burnt offerings and sacrifices, as in obeying the voice of the LORD? Behold, to obey is better than sacrifice, and to hearken than the fat of rams. [23] For rebellion is as the sin of witchcraft, and stubbornness is as iniquity and idolatry. Because thou hast rejected the word of the LORD, he hath also rejected thee from being king. (1 Samuel 15:18-23 KJV)

Just as rebellion is costly, ignorance is deadly. Both were at play in my adulterous relationship. I had met this guy at work, and I was doing things with this guy that would have led me straight to hell. I had become another person. He would say certain things to me that nobody ever knew, as if a devil was prophesying to me. I would think, "Okay, how do you know that?" Then I would brush it off. The more I was around this person, the more I would get heavy, heavy dreams. I even had a dream about him trying to cast a spell on me. "I'm 'gonna put a hex on you," he said in the dream. And I said, "What is that?" It was crazy. I would dream about him having an altar with my picture on it. The more God began to deal with me, the more he showed me that this person was doing evil things. This guy was someone I worked with; we were in the same division at my job.

In another dream, his hand was black, and the Holy Spirit said, "That's a binding." In yet another dream, there were snakes going toward him. I asked, "Holy Spirit, what is that?" The Holy Spirit said, "He comes from a family of witches and warlocks," and I said, "That's what it is—witchcraft!" What he was doing finally hit me. Finally, my spiritual eyes opened! Thank God for his mercy. I had finally gotten the revelation.

The price of ignorance is extremely high. A lot of time went by, and a lot of damage had been done by the time I realized what had been going on. In these days in times, we cannot afford to be ignorant of the enemy's devices. So, no matter how strange it may or may not sound to you, trust me when I tell you that witchcraft is real. Evil is real, and it targets the righteous. It targets those with a call and assignment. Proverbs 6:26b KJV says, "…the adultress will hunt for the precious life." That wicked spirit targets the precious life. Evil targets good. So, refuse to be ignorant because it could cost you something very precious.

> REFUSE TO BE IGNORANT
> BECAUSE IT COULD COST

YOU SOMETHING VERY PRECIOUS.

When God began restoring me, he prompted me to study and do research. It is difficult to be delivered from an enemy you don't understand. That's why I'm so glad that you have chosen to read this book and increase your knowledge concerning the operations of witchcraft, curses, narcissism, and the spirit of jezebel.

Knowledge is an antidote for ignorance but specifically, the knowledge of God. James 3:15 says that there is wisdom that is not heavenly but instead earthly, sensual, and devilish. In the battle against witchcraft and all the operations of the enemy, we need the knowledge of God, the knowledge that comes from heaven and is imparted by the spirit of God. For the Holy Spirit is the spirit of knowledge, understanding, wisdom, the fear of the Lord, counsel, and might, according to Isaiah 11:2. The knowledge of God is the knowledge that was missing and led to the destruction of God's people—not earthly wisdom.

- Hear the word of the LORD, You children of Israel, For the LORD *brings* a charge against the inhabitants of the land: "There is no truth or mercy **Or knowledge of God** in the land. **⁶ My people are destroyed for lack of knowledge**. Because you have rejected knowledge, I also will reject you from being priest for Me; Because you have forgotten the law of your God, I also will forget your children. ⁷ "The more they increased, The more they sinned against Me; I will change their glory into shame. ⁸ They eat up the sin of My people; They set their heart on their iniquity. ⁹ And it shall be: like people, like priest. So I will punish them for their ways, And reward them for their deeds. ¹⁰ For they shall eat, but not have enough; They shall commit harlotry, but not increase; Because they have ceased obeying the LORD. (Hosea 4:1, 6-10 NKJV, emphasis added)

- They spend their days in wealth, and in a moment go down to the grave. [14] Therefore they say unto God, Depart from us; for **we desire not the knowledge of thy ways**. (Job 21:13-14 KJV)
- Oh, **the depth of the riches both of the wisdom and knowledge of God**! How unsearchable *are* His judgments and His ways past finding out! [34] "For who has known the mind of the LORD? Or who has become His counselor?" [35] "Or who has first given to Him And it shall be repaid to him?" [36] For of Him and through Him and to Him *are* all things, to whom *be* glory forever. Amen. (Romans 11:33-36 NKJV)

Chapter Recap

Here are some key things to remember from this chapter concerning ignorance:

- The media has desensitized us to the realities of witchcraft and the potency of the powers that back its activities. The Wiccans and satanists are organized, recognized religions that are growing in number every day in the United States (US). According to a 2018 article by Pew Research, there were an estimated 1.5 million Wicca or Pagans in the US, which means that witches outnumber Presbyterians in America.[4]
- There are examples of witchcraft and both the Old and New Testaments.
- Breaking any law or commandment of God has consequences, especially when we are walking in ignorance of the enemy's devices.

---

[4] Pew Research Center. "Religious Landscape Study." Pewresearch.org. Accessed July 6, 2022. https://www.pewresearch.org/religion/religious-landscape-study/religious-denomination/pagan-or-wiccan/.

- The definition of ignorance (*noun*) is the state or fact of being **ignorant**, lack of knowledge, learning, information, etc.[5]
- So many Christians rush into relationships without taking the time to study and investigate the person. It is so dangerous, yet we often don't take the necessary time to know a person before opening up our emotions and giving our bodies to someone.
- Through knowledge the just are delivered (Proverbs 11:9b KJV).
- There was so much relief after I fasted correctly. Knowledge of God's ways is key.
- Witchcraft also comes in the form of rebellion, manipulation, domination, and control. Anytime you alter or try to alter someone's destiny, try to control

---

[5] Dictionary.com, s.v. "Definition of ignorance (noun)," accessed July 6, 2022, https://www.dictionary.com/browse/ignorance

someone—any time you turn someone's "no" into your "yes," that is witchcraft.

- The price of ignorance is extremely high. A lot of time went by, and a lot of damage had been done by the time I realized what had been going on. In these days in times, we cannot afford to be ignorant of the enemy's devices.
- When God began restoring me, he prompted me to study and do research. It is difficult to be delivered from an enemy you don't understand.
- Knowledge is an antidote for ignorance but specifically, the knowledge of God.

In the next chapter, we explore the important topic of generational curses. I had to confront this topic because the issues that affected my marriage were issues my mother had to deal with in her marriage. They were not new. Recurring issues and negative patterns are an indication of generational curses. In chapter two, we define generational curses, examine examples, and discuss how the Word of

God says we can deal with them. Thank God for victory, in Jesus' name.

CHAPTER 2: GENERATIONAL CURSES

> LIKE A FLUTTERING SPARROW OR A DARTING SWALLOW, AN UNDESERVED CURSE DOES NOT COME TO REST.
> (PROVERBS 26:2 NIV)

There are spiritual reasons for what we see repeatedly happening in our families and lives. I thank God that I received deliverance. Yes, thank God for deliverance. He changed me from the inside out and delivered me. Oh, how we need to appropriate our deliverance through the blood of Jesus. The problem is we may not even know we need it, and if we discover that we need it, we may not know how to materialize it or enforce it. I never knew generational curses were tied to what was manifesting in my life, specifically what was manifesting in my marriage.

Many people find themselves in that state. They meet someone they genuinely love, and perhaps, things are good for a while. Then, suddenly, there is offense and misunderstanding followed by constant strife. They begin to argue about the most trivial things and can't stand the sight of one another. They start looking for solace in other people and soon don't even want to be around the person they used to love. Eventually, they don't even care about their initial commitment—they just want out! The person they once genuinely loved now feels like their enemy. It's not natural, right? That's right. It's not natural: It's spiritual.

It is so important to realize that what goes on in life here on earth is spiritual. The spiritual realm is real. Look at what these Scriptures say about the spiritual realm:

> So we fix our eyes not on what is seen, but on what is unseen, since what is seen is

temporary, but what is unseen is eternal. (2 Corinthians 4:18 NIV)

For our struggle is not against flesh and blood, but against the rulers, against the authorities, against the powers of this dark world and against the spiritual forces of evil in the heavenly realms. (Ephesians 6:12 NIV)

> IT IS SO IMPORTANT TO REALIZE THAT WHAT GOES ON IN LIFE HERE ON EARTH IS SPIRITUAL. THE SPIRITUAL REALM IS REAL.

If you think about it, living without a reality of the spiritual realm is very dangerous. It means you could be fighting and struggling in life without knowing who the right target is or who's your real opponent. In marriage, you start fighting each other instead of the real enemy. Or, in life, you could be fighting but only beating the air, fighting in a fruitless effort because you are not aware of the real source behind your problem. Again, ignorance is extremely costly. God said his people are destroyed because of lack of knowledge—his people are destroyed because of ignorance. And we cannot afford to be ignorant of what's really the source of what happens in our families and marriages.

Defining a Generational Curse by Example

According to Ephesians 6:12, if we are struggling, it means we are struggling against something, but it's not what we see with our natural eyes. It says, "our struggle is not against flesh and blood." Things were happening in my family and my marriage, but I didn't realize the source of the struggle. To further explain, let me give you an example of the "struggles" I finally identified in my family.

Women in my family never married, and the guys they were with would never stick around. I observed this first-hand in my mom's life and in my aunts'. None of them are married. No one has a husband. Yet, all of them have a "baby daddy."

That same thing has occurred in their children's lives and in their children's, children's lives. It has repeated itself, and that's a sign of a curse.

> One of illegitimate birth shall not enter the assembly of the LORD; even to the tenth generation none of his *descendants* shall enter the assembly of the LORD.
> (Deuteronomy 23:2 NKJV, emphasis added)

THAT SAME THING HAS OCCURRED IN THEIR CHILDREN'S LIVES AND IN THEIR CHILDREN'S, CHILDREN'S LIVES. IT HAS REPEATED ITSELF AND THAT'S A SIGN OF A CURSE.

This Scripture tells us that under the Old Covenant, committing fornication and conceiving a child from that fornication brought a curse. The Scripture says the child born from fornication (unmarried parents) is affected by a curse. It seems unfair, but wait—it's even more serious. The child's descendants were also affected. It means that for generations, a family can see a pattern taking place. They can see generation after generation of children failing and not understand that there is an unseen force working against them, that an unseen law is in operation against that family. Why? What sets the unseen law in motion? It is because the parents' sinned; they violated the Lord's command. There are consequences to sin in the spirit realm and in the natural. And when it is a sin that invokes a curse, the result is that a pattern is created, something is repeated, and it's not good. Something spiritual goes into motion to ensure the pattern remains.

The Old Testament defines fornication as harlotry. It calls a fornicator a harlot, the word from which we derive the modern-day expression "ho." The Urban Dictionary defines a ho as a prostitute, whore, hooker, tramp, slut. Interestingly enough, the Old Testament had already set a precedent. Look at these verses and how they describe Tamar's actions:

> And it came to pass, about three months after, that Judah was told, saying, "Tamar your daughter-in-law has *played the harlot*; furthermore she *is* with child by *harlotry*." So Judah said, "Bring her out and let her be burned!" (Genesis 38:24 NKJV, emphasis added)

> Lo! soothly after three months they told to Judah, and said, Tamar, thy son's wife, *hath done fornication*, and her womb seemeth to wax great. Judah said, Bring her forth, (so) that she (can) be burnt(!). (Genesis 38:24 Wycliffe Bible, emphasis added)

> And it cometh to pass about three months [after], that it is declared to Judah, saying, `Tamar thy daughter-in-law hath *committed fornication*; and also, lo, she hath *conceived by fornication*:' and Judah saith, `Bring her out -- and she is burnt.' (Genesis 38:24 Young's Literal Translation, emphasis added)

Tamar's fornication is described as harlotry. Pay close attention to the fact that they were about to put Tamar to death—to burn her alive—for her harlotry. That means she and the child she was pregnant with would die. Fornication brought the curse of death under the Old Covenant. They didn't see it as a sin that only affected the two people who lay down together to have sex. They understood that it affected the two people, the child the woman got pregnant with, and the land (the atmosphere) where they lived.

> Look up to the barren heights and see. Is there any place where you have not been ravished? By the roadside you sat waiting for lovers, sat like a nomad in the desert. You have defiled the land with your prostitution and wickedness. (Jeremiah 3:2 NIV)

This should really help people to understand that fornication, having "baby daddies," and repeatedly seeing children born to unmarried parents is a serious thing. Someone in the family must speak up and say this has to stop. It cannot become the normal thing to do. No wonder the New Testament speaks so strongly against it. It has damaging effects. Consider these Scriptures:

> Flee from sexual immorality. All other sins a person commits are outside the body, but

> whoever sins sexually, sins against their own body. (1 Corinthians 6:18 NIV)
>
> It is God's will that you should be sanctified: that you should avoid sexual immorality; that each of you should learn to control your own body in a way that is holy and honorable, not in passionate lust like the pagans, who do not know God. (1 Thessalonians 4:3-5 NIV)
>
> You must abstain from eating food offered to idols, from consuming blood or the meat of strangled animals, and from sexual immorality. If you do this, you will do well. Farewell. (Acts 15:29 NLT)
>
> Now the body is not for fornication, but for the Lord; and the Lord for the body. 1 (Corinthians 6:12 KJV)
>
> We must not indulge in sexual immorality as some of them did, and twenty-three thousand fell in a single day. (1 Corinthians 10:8 ESV)

The child conceived from fornication was cast out of the congregation of the Lord, and the parents, if caught, we put to death. Either way, the parents and the children were cut off from something and kept from enjoying life. A curse keeps you from enjoying some good things in life you are supposed to enjoy. It keeps you from enjoying the abundant life in Christ in one area or another or several areas. The New Testament says it this way:

> Know ye not that the unrighteous shall not inherit the kingdom of God? Be not deceived: ***neither fornicators***, nor idolaters, nor adulterers, nor effeminate, nor abusers of themselves with mankind, [10] Nor thieves, nor covetous, nor drunkards, nor revilers, nor extortioners, shall inherit the kingdom of God. (1 Corinthians 6:9-10 KJV, emphasis added)

> But the fearful, and unbelieving, and the abominable, and murderers, and ***whoremongers***, and sorcerers, and idolaters, and all liars, shall have their part in the lake which burneth with fire and brimstone: which is the second death. (Revelation 21:8 KJV, emphasis added)

A CURSE KEEPS YOU FROM ENJOYING SOME GOOD THINGS IN LIFE YOU ARE SUPPOSED TO ENJOY. IT KEEPS YOU FROM

ENJOYING THE ABUNDANT LIFE IN CHRIST IN ONE AREA OR ANOTHER OR SEVERAL AREAS.

Another thing I observed in my family was poverty. As I grew up, I saw my mom and a few family members working here and there, but then I also saw them quit their jobs frequently. No one seemed to keep a job. They were not stable in that area. Instead, they would be on welfare or subsidized housing, and they just stayed in it. It was okay to them; no one seemed to see anything wrong with living that way. That's the trick of the enemy; God never wants us to stay there. I see how it followed from one generation to the next. I saw it in the newer generation of my family, the younger ones.

The Scriptures are very clear about poverty. Poverty is listed as part of the curse of the law in Deuteronomy 28:38-40, 43-45.

> Thou shalt carry much seed out into the field, and shalt gather but little in; for the locust shall consume it. [39] Thou shalt plant

vineyards, and dress them, but shalt neither drink of the wine, nor gather the grapes; for the worms shall eat them. ⁴⁰ Thou shalt have olive trees throughout all thy coasts, but thou shalt not anoint thyself with the oil; for thine olive shall cast his fruit.
(Deuteronomy 28:38-40 KJV)

The stranger that is within thee shall get up above thee very high; and thou shalt come down very low. ⁴⁴ He shall lend to thee, and thou shalt not lend to him: he shall be the head, and thou shalt be the tail. ⁴⁵ Moreover *all these curses* shall come upon thee, and shall pursue thee, and overtake thee, till thou be destroyed; because thou hearkenedst not unto the voice of the LORD thy God, to keep his commandments and his statutes which he commanded thee (Deuteronomy 28:43-45 KJV, emphasis added)

The patterns of sowing much but reaping little, seeing what you have devoured, or not being able to lend but always borrowing are all curses. Poverty is a curse. Poverty means:

- The state or condition of having little or no money, goods, or means of support; the condition of being poor.
- The condition of being without adequate food, money, etc.
- Deficiency of necessary or desirable ingredients, qualities, etc.
- Scantiness; insufficiency
- Scarcity or dearth
- A lack of elements conducive to fertility in land or soil[6]

This is definitely not the state that we are supposed to be in or that Jesus would have us stay. Yet still, I saw poverty in my family.

Something was wrong, but I didn't realize it right away. No, unfortunately, I didn't. For me to catch this and grab it, I had to go through some things. In 2019, God said to me that I had to go through

---

[6] Oxford Dictionary, s.v. "Definition poverty (noun)," accessed September 12, 2022, https://www.dictionary.com/browse/poverty.

some things to receive instruction and become a deliverer.

I can now look back and see that God's hands were on me throughout everything I went through. He was there the whole entire time. And it's so amazing that earlier that year, my mom came and told me that I was the one that was supposed to go through it.

I felt like my family members needed to seek God for themselves, and it is true that they do. But God needed someone to show them these things about the generational curses in our family. I felt like I was going through so much—too much to be overwhelmed with their problems too. But what I went through wasn't just for my understanding but also for the sake of others. God spoke to me and said, "Except you go through it, how can you help someone else."

It is Spiritual

He had to speak to me and help me understand that what was happening was spiritual. Had I not come to understand that it was spiritual, I would have never known how to fight. If what is fighting you is spiritual, then you must get into the Word of God to fight back.

Thankfully, God also spoke to me in a dream. In this dream, I saw several family members. There was a group that represented an older generation. I saw my mom, some other cousins, and another set of cousins in front of me. There were different generations of my family there.

I was in a room in a bed, and my cousins were in their different beds. And spirits began to come and go around to check different family members in their beds. As they checked, they would take different family members. When the spirits came to me, they moved on and took another family member instead. One of my family members sat up in her bed and said, pray.

I ended up in the bathroom and then on a beach. The spirits were pulling and taking whoever belonged to them. I saw this person that I knew in the dream. I knew they were a bad person. They were saying their goodbyes. And I woke up, and the Spirit said, "He's checking." Thank God the bad person had to say goodbye. That's how I knew the enemy sends familiar spirits to check to see who they can take in the family and continue the pattern of the curse. That's how I knew that what was going on in my life, my marriage, and my family was spiritual.

Once I became aware that this fight was a spiritual fight, then I could use the right weapons and have a better chance of winning, versus me just going about my business ignorantly. If you take the wrong weapons to a battle, you are bound to lose. The weapons of our warfare are not carnal. So if you take carnal weapons into a spiritual battle for your marriage or family, you are bound to lose. The curse that enforces patterns of divorce against the marriages in your family will continue to win. But if you use the right weapons, you have a fighting chance.

> For though we walk in the flesh, we do not war after the flesh: 4 (For the weapons of our warfare are not carnal, but mighty through God to the pulling down of strong holds;) 5 Casting down imaginations, and every high thing that exalteth itself against the knowledge of God, and bringing into captivity every thought to the obedience of Christ; (2 Corinthians 10:3-5 KJV)

For us to fight and win, we have to go to the Word of God because it's spiritual. The things that are manifesting naturally have already occurred spiritually.

Know the Word

The enemy is a legalist, meaning he wants to use the penalties of breaking God's law against you. He knows the Word of God, he lived in heaven, and he knows the way God operates. He will use what your family members have done in the past to anger God against your present because he is the accuser of the brethren.

> And I heard a loud voice saying in heaven, Now is come salvation, and strength, and

> the kingdom of our God, and the
> power of his Christ: for
> the accuser of our brethren is cast down,
> which accused them before our God day
> and night. (Revelation 12:10 KJV)

If he is accusing you before God day and night, what exactly is he saying? What is it that he is taking to God to raise an accusation against you twice a day? The devil will search your family line for discrepancies. So part of his accusations against you are to demand payment for the wrongs your family members have done.

For example, idolatry angers God. He is a jealous God and hates idolatry. If your family members were involved in idolatry, the devil can use that as an accusation against you to reason with God that your family should not be blessed because of what they did. But just like in a court of law, you must have something to say in objection to the accusation. If your family members were indeed guilty, what will you say?

You must know the Word of God in order to have the right defense against the accusation and revoke the enemy's right to use your family's sins against you. You must know that "Christ hath redeemed us from the curse of the law, being made a curse for us: for it is written, Cursed is every one that hangeth on a tree" (Galatians 3:13 KJV). You have to speak your defense and break the curse.

I can now teach my family these things and help them to understand what is happening and what has been happening in our family for years. Whatever I went through, it was not only for me to learn and be delivered but also to help my family. You may be going through a lot, but God will deliver you as well, and you will also be able to deliver others. Know the Word of God, and be proactive.

Be Proactive

Now that you know that the enemy wants to use things in your family background to impose curses, be proactive. Begin to identify patterns.

What's repeating itself in your family that should not? What has to stop? The Word of God gives us leverage over the enemy's accusations. But if you sit quietly in court and don't bring reasonable doubt against your accuser, you will lose the case even if you're innocent. You must raise your objection with the Word of God. Don't wait for things to keep happening.

> Be sober, be vigilant; because your adversary the devil, as a roaring lion, walketh about, seeking whom he may devour. (1 Peter 5:8 KJV)

I thank God that I am helping my family move forward from those things, and I know that if God did it for me, he can also do it for you. You are blessed beyond the curse.

Chapter Recap

Here are some key things to remember from this chapter concerning generational curses:

- They create a pattern of recurring issues in a family.

- They keep you from enjoying the abundant life Christ died for you to enjoy.
- They bring poverty.
- They are spiritual.
- Someone must stand up and break them with the power of the Word.

In the next chapter, we discuss the topic of narcissism. I encountered narcissism first-hand when I was dating the guy at my job. He was extremely controlling and wanted things his way. These were symptoms of narcissism, but I didn't know it at the time. God brought me through the fire. Let's continue as the Holy Spirit empowers us to deal with narcissism, the spirit of jezebel, and witchcraft.

CHAPTER 3: NARCISSISM

Charm. Cruelty. Charisma. Control. All these words describe the two-sided nature of the narcissist. To better understand the narcissist, you might think of the book, *Strange Case of Dr. Jekyll and Mr. Hyde* by Robert Louis Stevenson. This book details the life of an otherwise good scientist who dabbles in the dark side of science to bring out a second nature or alter ego. There were two sides of the same person, and the phrase Dr. Jekyll and Mr. Hyde is often used to refer to:

- a person or thing that alternately displays two different sides to their character or nature

- one having a two-sided personality, one side of which is good and the other evil[7]

The narcissist is much like Dr. Jekyll and Mr. Hyde. They can be charming, but mainly to the end that they get what they want. They are full of charisma, and people love them, yet they can be controlling and verbally abusive when they are challenged or called out on their inconsistencies. Rev. David Wilson Rogers explains the narcissist this way:

> The challenge is that a narcissist is frequently very charismatic and has an uncanny ability to win people over to his or her side. The narcissist knows how to attract people to them, say what they want to hear, and convince them that the narcissist has their best interests at heart. Yet, it is a dangerous trap. In spite of outward appearances to the contrary, the narcissist is only concerned about him or

---

[7] Merriam-Webster, s.v. "Definition Jekyll and Hyde (noun)," accessed September 12, 2022. https://www.merriam-webster.com/dictionary/Jekyll%20and%20Hyde.

herself and getting people to uphold the narcissist as a perfect person deserving of unquestioned loyalty. The narcissist will distort truth, make up lies, and reinterpret the past in order to save face and look good to those from whom the narcissist demands loyalty. This revision of reality generally makes the narcissist look larger than life, glosses over any faults, shortcomings, or mistakes, and creates an image that the narcissist is beyond comparison in perfection. The narcissist will also hijack other people's successes and hard work in order to claim credit and adulation for themselves. Worse yet, most narcissists are haplessly oblivious to the false reality they try to create about themselves and genuinely believe their own false perspective, so they expect others to buy into it as well. When that fails to happen, those who question or challenge the narcissist are punished, degraded, and humiliated as being fake. Incapable of seeing past their own delusional need for control and power, and being the center of the universe, narcissists will unwittingly destroy their family, friendships, and associations while blaming the failures on anyone and anything beyond themselves.

Unwilling to accept responsibility for their own actions, they will form allegiances with those in their realm of influence to isolate, degrade, blame, and even harm those who fail to show the allegiance they deem vital to their narcissistic needs.[8]

If you ever find yourself in a relationship with a narcissist, you're in a danger zone. They will lure you in with charm, but they will also have the witchcraft tendencies of domination, control, and retaliation. They are the kind of person who will abuse you and treat you like you are inferior yet not want anyone else to have you. It's all about them; they don't want to love you unless you can get them some status or applause. They just want to control you so that you continue to serve their agenda.

> IF YOU EVER FIND
> YOURSELF IN A

---

[8] Rev. David Wilson Rogers, "Battling narcissism and its dangers with faith," September 3, 2020, Carlsbad Current Argus, Currentargus.com, accessed September 12, 2022. https://www.currentargus.com/story/life/faith/2020/09/13/battling-narcissism-and-its-dangers-faith/3457531001/.

RELATIONSHIP WITH A NARCISSIST, YOU'RE IN A DANGER ZONE.

Think about cult leaders like Jim Jones and others who have lured and deceived people into believing that they are some kind of savior. This is the kind of charm and manipulation characteristic of a narcissist. A narcissist spirit is a Luciferian spirit. Remember, Lucifer carried away a third of the angels from heaven to follow him. He was all about himself, just as a narcissist is all about themself.

> How art thou fallen from heaven, O Lucifer, son of the morning! how art thou cut down to the ground, which didst weaken the nations! [13] For thou hast said in thine heart, *I will* ascend into heaven, *I will* exalt my throne above the stars of God: *I will* sit also upon the mount of the congregation, in the sides of the north: [14] *I will ascend* above the heights of the clouds; I will be like the most High. (Isaiah 14:12-14 KJV, emphasis added)

Please take note that "I will" is repeated in the passage of Scripture. Lucifer's selfishness and self-centeredness are reflected in the use of the phrase "I will." Lucifer was all about himself. That's why narcissists usually look for overly-submissive, blindly loyal, or hurt and rejected people for their romantic relationships. They want to stay on the throne. They want to maintain a perfect image of themselves, and they need constant admiration, or they turn antagonistic.

The trap of the narcissist is that you don't see the dark side and control until after you are taken by their charm and flattery. Remember, "the narcissist knows how to attract people to them, say what they want to hear, and convince them that the narcissist has their best interests at heart."[9] This is manipulation, and you can be manipulated and not know what is happening. Manipulation is a hallmark of witchcraft. Another variant of manipulation is seduction, and anyone who

---

[9] Ibid.

operates in a spirit of narcissism can also operate in seduction. Both manipulation and seduction aim to get another person to bend to their own selfish desires. A narcissist is all about self, but their charm masks their selfishness. Others are blind to it until they get close and recognize the patterns. And if they do recognize and call the narcissist out on it, they become the target of the narcissist's rage, mood swings, and verbal abuse.

> In spite of outward appearances to the contrary, the narcissist is only concerned about him or herself and getting people to uphold the narcissist as a perfect person deserving of unquestioned loyalty. The narcissist will distort truth, make up lies, and reinterpret the past in order to save face and look good to those from whom the narcissist demands loyalty.[10]

Psychology has focused on narcissism as a disorder. However, the Bible gives us an example

---

[10] Ibid.

of what a narcissist might look like in Matthew 18:21-35 KJV:

> Then came Peter to him, and said, Lord, how oft shall my brother sin against me, and I forgive him? till seven times? ²² Jesus saith unto him, I say not unto thee, Until seven times: but, Until seventy times seven. ²³ Therefore is the kingdom of heaven likened unto a certain king, which would take account of his servants. ²⁴ And when he had begun to reckon, one was brought unto him, which owed him ten thousand talents. ²⁵ But forasmuch as he had not to pay, his lord commanded him to be sold, and his wife, and children, and all that he had, and payment to be made. ²⁶ The servant therefore fell down, and worshipped him, saying, Lord, have patience with me, and I will pay thee all. ²⁷ Then the lord of that servant was moved with compassion, and loosed him, and forgave him the debt. ²⁸ But the same servant went out, and found one of his fellowservants, which owed him an hundred pence: and he laid hands on him, and took him by the throat, saying, Pay me that thou owest. ²⁹ And his fellowservant fell down at his feet, and besought him,

saying, Have patience with me, and I will pay thee all. ³⁰ And he would not: but went and cast him into prison, till he should pay the debt. ³¹ So when his fellowservants saw what was done, they were very sorry, and came and told unto their lord all that was done. ³² Then his lord, after that he had called him, said unto him, O thou wicked servant, I forgave thee all that debt, because thou desiredst me: ³³ Shouldest not thou also have had compassion on thy fellowservant, even as I had pity on thee? ³⁴ And his lord was wroth, and delivered him to the tormentors, till he should pay all that was due unto him. ³⁵ So likewise shall my heavenly Father do also unto you, if ye from your hearts forgive not every one his brother their trespasses.

Here are some characteristics of narcissists we can see from Matthew 18:21-35. A narcissist:

- Uses the severest form of judgment on others while demanding the strongest form of grace from others.
    - The servant in this parable owed his master much more than his friend

owed him. The servant wanted grace but was unwilling to extend any grace to his friend, who owed him money. Narcissists expect and somehow believe they deserve preferential treatment, that the rules that apply to them are different than the rules everyone else must follow. In their minds, they are in a class of their own. This is where their confidence comes from, which is often attractive. But it's also where their cruel arrogance and lack of empathy come from, which is destructive.

- Will have crazy mood swings, which are used as an attempt to control others.
    - He grabbed his friend, who owed him money, by the throat. Where did all that rage come from after just having been forgiven for his own debts? It's like a switch was flipped.

> The same devil that will seduce you will kill you.

- Will often be marked by false humility, especially when they claim to be a Christian.[11]
  - The servant was so humble when it came to his own situation but cruel to someone else's. Where was his humility when his friend was begging him for mercy?

Please, please, please take note of the warning signs. When you recognize them, don't attach yourself to someone with a narcissistic spirit.

Narcissism can also develop from a place of hurt or pain in childhood as a masking and protective mechanism. The narcissistic person often targets people in pain—broken, hurt people recognize other broken and hurt people. However, the

---

[11] Mark Ballenger, "What Does the Bible Say About Narcissism? (16 Signs)," Apply God's Word, accessed September 12, 2022. https://applygodsword.com/what-does-the-bible-say-about-narcissism-16-signs/.

narcissistic person sees the hurt person as easy prey. I recognized this while in the "situationship" with the guy on my job. I had just broken off a relationship with another person and came to a realization of the narcissistic spirit operating through the guy at my job. My brokenness and hurt attracted this spirit.

Chapter Recap

Here are some key things to remember from this chapter concerning narcissists, they:

- Can be charming, but mainly to the end that they get what they want.
- Are full of charisma, and people love them, yet they can be controlling and verbally abusive when they are challenged or called out on their inconsistencies.
- Will lure you in with charm, but they will also have the witchcraft tendencies of domination, control, and retaliation.

- Are the kind of person who will abuse you and treat you like you are inferior yet not want anyone else to have you.

In the next chapter, we explore the spirit of jezebel, which is closely connected to the narcissist. In many narcissistic traits is a manifestation of the spirit of jezebel. Let's continue.

CHAPTER 4: JEZEBEL

In 2020, the Lord helped me to identify the jezebel spirit. That spirit operated through the person with whom I was in a destructive relationship. Little did I know, the jezebel spirit is attracted to hurt, fear, and those who are in emotional pain. It's common for the jezebel spirit to attack those who experienced early pain, typically that started from childhood where the child's innocence was stolen, or they were significantly affected emotionally, causing them to disconnect.

He knew that I was hurt and in pain. One day he said, "I knew you before you knew me. I saw you first." I didn't understand that. However, afterward, I realized that, through him, this spirit used manipulation in a major way, which is a form of witchcraft. Manipulating people and circumstances to control others is demonic. Jezebel used manipulation to get Naboth's vineyard (1 Kings 21:11). She lied and used fear, violence, and the threat of violence to control others.

Manipulation is the act of manipulating to get something you want; it's a skillful control. It can be used in forms of flattery, isolation, devaluation, fear, or violence. I experienced all this while in this relationship. He was very cunning, and it was very similar to how the serpent manipulated Eve in the garden.

> The serpent was the shrewdest of all the wild animals the LORD God had made. One day he asked the woman, "Did God really say you must not eat the fruit from any of the trees in the garden?" 2 "Of course we may eat fruit from the trees in the garden," the woman replied. 3 "It's only the fruit from the tree in the middle of the garden that we are not allowed to eat. God said,

> 'You must not eat it or even touch it; if you do, you will die.'" ⁴ "You won't die!" the serpent replied to the woman. ⁵ "God knows that your eyes will be opened as soon as you eat it, and you will be like God, knowing both good and evil." ⁶ The woman was convinced. She saw that the tree was beautiful and its fruit looked delicious, and she wanted the wisdom it would give her. So she took some of the fruit and ate it. Then she gave some to her husband, who was with her, and he ate it, too. ⁷ At that moment their eyes were opened, and they suddenly felt shame at their nakedness. So they sewed fig leaves together to cover themselves. (Genesis 3:1-7 NLT)
>
> Then the LORD God asked the woman, "What have you done?" "The serpent deceived me," she replied. "That's why I ate it." (Genesis 3:13 NLT)

Manipulation is very demonic; it's the enemy himself. The enemy poses as an angel of light. Similarly, narcissistic, jezebelic people wear masks. They come under the guise of charm, but their aim is destructive. This was only revealed to me over the course of time as I got to know him. Little things would come to me—I began to see and hear certain things, and God gave me understanding.

This person once said, "I'm going to do whatever I want to do, and you're 'gonna just take it." We had gone into the house, and he said something similar again. So, I left. I jumped and walked out his door. I could feel him walking behind me and knew he wanted to do me harm because he would always make threats. He spewed out threats and word curses. I didn't initially recognize what he was saying as such, but Jezebel spews out word curses.

He was very jealous, manipulative, flattering, cunning, and controlling to get whatever he wanted. That is how that spirit operates. I saw him do this even with his own children at times.

To get deliverance, I had to repent and come out of agreement with that spirit. I could feel a pull at my heart, and God began to show me the spirit in this person.

That evil spirit knew that I was leaving and tried to do everything to stop me. He began to spread lies on the job; I was with this person every single day on the job. I later found out he was casting spells and doing sorcery and witchcraft against me. One day he mentioned something about his grandfather being a witch doctor. And I had a dream that he had an altar.

We don't realize these things are real. Just because you don't see it, you can't assume it's not happening, or it's not real. Remember, God said, "my people perish through lack of knowledge." Ignorance is costly, and jezebel is attracted to ignorance. To my own demise, my ignorance was helping this spirit.

In the midst of my deliverance—as I was trying to leave the relationship—God began to show me these things. This spirit would try to attack me in so many ways with intimidation, threats, and every way possible. I didn't realize that this spirit wore many hats. When I was with this person, I would always tell him, "You're a narcissist." But I didn't realize what I was really saying.

The enemy was trying to shift me and change me. He wanted to become like the guy I was in a relationship with so I would not walk in kingdom authority.

I had to recognize that I was in error for being in the relationship in the first place. I had to repent and turn away from all of it, including some family members, so I could acknowledge and understand where I was in error.

> From that time Jesus began to preach, and to say, Repent: for the kingdom of heaven is at hand. (Matthew 4:17 KJV)
>
> But if we confess our sins to him, he is faithful and just to forgive us our sins and to cleanse us from all wickedness. (1 John 1:9 NLT)

God had to take me through a whole process. He led me on a fast. I wasn't raised in the Church, so I didn't have extensive knowledge. I had gone to prayer, so I had heard of some Scriptures. And one day, I heard in my head, "These kinds come out only by fasting and prayer."

> Then came the disciples to Jesus apart, and said, Why could not we cast him out? [20] And Jesus said unto them, Because of your unbelief: for verily I say unto you, If ye have faith as a grain of mustard seed, ye shall say unto this mountain, Remove hence to yonder place; and it shall remove; and nothing shall be impossible unto you. [21] Howbeit this kind goeth not out but by prayer and fasting. (Matthew 17:19-21 KJV)

When I heard that Scripture in my mind, I Googled it, and that started my ten-day fast. I was desperate. During that time, I heard, "drink and eat." I didn't know if it was God or the devil, so I was just determined to keep fasting and praying. I heard again, "drink and eat." I was very ill but slowly began to eat and drink. I would make soup from bouillon cubes. After I did that, the Lord showed me how to properly fast and pray through a pastor who was teaching about Isaiah 58. This is key to defeating this spirit because these kinds come not out except by fasting and prayer. It's a spiritual fight.

> (For the weapons of our warfare are not carnal, but mighty through God to the pulling down of strong holds;) [5] Casting down imaginations, and every high thing that exalteth itself against the knowledge of God, and bringing into captivity every thought to the obedience of Christ; (2 Corinthians 10:4-5 KJV)

When I understood 2 Corinthians 10:5, it became my go-to Scripture. Anytime an attack would come, or this person would come around me, I would quote this Scripture, and he would shift or leave.

Getting away from him and coming out of agreement with that spirit was a major deliverance for me.

It piqued my interest even more, and as I read the story of Ahab and Jezebel in the Bible, I understood that spirit is attracted to fear, disobedience, and power. Also, when someone relinquishes their God-given authority, it also attracts that spirit. That's not to put this spirit in a box. These are things the Lord highlighted to me as ways this spirit once ruled my life. The jezebel spirit is always in pursuit of God's people. I read many books in relation to this spirit and the connection to narcissistic behavior (narcissism).

Even in my own ignorance, I unknowingly and unintentionally invited that spirit. So whether a person knows it or not, they can still invite the kingdom of darkness to rule over their life. Not to mention, I grew up with a family full of narcissists or some type of narcissist behavior (Deuteronomy 28:15-20, Hosea 4:6). We are held accountable either way.

So it's important to understand this wicked spirit. Anytime there's manipulation or narcissism involved, the spirit of jezebel is operating. And the jezebel spirit is not female nor male—it's a spirit and can operate through males and females if allowed. Jezebel operates by plotting, scheming, lying, organizing demonic fasts, and manipulating to get what it wants.

Jezebel wanted to murder Elijah. That spirit will turn to violence and murder when it doesn't get its way. This spirit is attracted to pain and wants to cause more damage and destroy God's people. The spirit of jezebel sought to kill Elijah and other prophets, and that spirit still seeks to kill and destroy today.

> For it was so, when Jezebel cut off the prophets of the LORD, that Obadiah took an hundred prophets, and hid them by fifty in a cave, and fed them with bread and water.) (1 Kings 18:4 KJV)

> And Ahab told Jezebel all that Elijah had done, and withal how he had slain all the prophets with the sword. ² Then Jezebel sent a messenger unto Elijah, saying, So let the gods do to me, and more also, if I make not thy life as the life of one of them by tomorrow about this time. (1 Kings 19:1-2 KJV)

The jezebel spirit does not want you to understand and walk in your God-given authority. It does not want you to know who you are in Christ Jesus. It can work through family members. Now, I'm able to recognize manipulation when it tries to work through family members.

God will empower you to recognize the enemy's operations and workings in your family. It is only in Christ that we find hope and deliverance. Witchcraft, curses, and the spirit of jezebel are real. I experienced their evil workings. Still, God has brought me through the fire, and he will do the same for you. Remember, the weapons of our warfare are not carnal, but they are mighty!

I want to leave you with this final testimony. As God was bringing me through deliverance from that adulterous relationship and setting me free from generational curses, narcissism, and the spirit of jezebel, he gave me an idea. I set a timer on my phone. Every five minutes, no matter where I was or what I was doing, my phone would vibrate. Or, if I was not at work and had the volume on, it would read and alert me with a Scripture to shift my mind back onto God.

It's quite interesting how the Lord did that for me because I wouldn't have ever thought to do that. But I was so bound and desperate at the same time. No matter if I was awake or asleep, every five minutes, I would hear something that would remind me of God's Word and shift my mind's focus back to him.

Like I said, I was desperate. I was in desperate need of freedom. I was in desperate need of deliverance, and I wanted it. Be desperate for God's deliverance, and he will deliver. The Scripture says, "The righteous cry, and the LORD heareth, and *delivereth* them out of all their troubles" (Psalm 34:17, italics added).

I have also taught my family to do this as well because the enemy bombards our minds as his weapon of attack. Still, if we renew our minds, they will no longer be the enemy's playground.

The fight is spiritual, and our weapons must be spiritual. I would have never thought about putting the Scripture alerts on my phone on my own, but that is one of the ways that God has shown me to come out of being bound. If he did it for me, he can do it for you. God brought me through the fire, and he will do the same for you, in Jesus' name.

ABOUT THE AUTHOR

Antoinette Lewis was born in Oakland, California, and raised by in single-parent home. She is the second oldest of six children and has been inspired by the perseverance of her mother. At times, her mother wanted to give up, but she instead encouraged and cared for many people. Antoinette thanks God for her salvation and lives to tell of his deliverance in her life.

www.ingramcontent.com/pod-product-compliance
Lightning Source LLC
Chambersburg PA
CBHW061731040426
42453CB00026B/903